IMAGINATIVE SOCIAL STUDIES ACTIVITIES FOR THE ELEMENTARY SCHOOL

SIDNEY W. TIEDT

assistant professor of elementary education
san jose state college
formerly principal of mountain view elementary school
anchorage, alaska

and

IRIS M. TIEDT

formerly supervisor of student teaching, university of oregon
elementary school instructor, anchorage, alaska

TEACHERS PRACTICAL PRESS, INC.

Robert L. Schain, Editor-in-Chief
Murray Polner, Associate Editor

THE TEACHERS PRACTICAL PRESS, INC. subscribes to the philosophy that the key to good teaching is to be found in the quality of the teacher himself. This being the case, we recognize the great value and need for today's educator to develop and maintain a continuing program of professional self-improvement through the acquisition of up-to-date teaching techniques. This practical help can be gained only by becoming knowledgeable about practices and methods which have been found useful and successful.

Our goal is to provide this vital area of practical information for all educators. We hope that our series will contribute to the improvement of the teacher and teaching.

Library of Congress Catalog Card Number: 63-14818

Copyright © Teachers Practical Press, Inc., 1964

CONTENTS

4

1

TEACHING CURRENT EVENTS

The study of current events should be more than a sharing period during which students contribute a motley assortment of news items. A variety of methods will serve to motivate the students' interest and will break the routine as the study continues through the year.

The teacher's interest and enthusiasm do much to emphasize the importance of studying current happenings in the world. Thought-provoking questions should be asked so that students learn to consider the background of the news reported.

In the selection of techniques for the teaching of current events the following criteria were used: (1) Does the technique stimulate the interest of the students? (2) Does the technique develop skills and increase student participation? Here are six teaching techniques which have been found to be successful in the presentation of current affairs:

- Student Reporting
- The Press Conference
- Contemporary Events Scrapbook
- People in the News
- News in Pictures
- The Contemporary Time Line

▶ Student reporting

One of the more commonly used techniques for studying current events is reporting by individual students. Each student is assigned a specific area on which to report. A short period is allotted each day for the reports of a group of students.

5

- *By Geographic Area.* One way this type of reporting can be organized is by dividing the class into committees with each committee assigned one day of the week on which to present reports. Each group may be given a specific geographic area on which to report, for example, local, regional, state, national, or international. These assignments should be rotated so that all students have an opportunity to investigate different areas. With this type of organization local news is covered one day each week, national news is reported one day a week, and so forth.

- *By Committee.* A variation of this type of organization is the use of daily committees. Each member of, for example, the Monday Committee is assigned to one of the geographic areas listed in the foregoing paragraph. Under this arrangement local news is reported on Monday by one person on that particular day's committee; national news is reported by another person; thus, all areas are covered each day. On Tuesday another group operates the same way.

- *By Individual Problems.* Another interesting way to organize news reporting is around the problem-centered report. After having explored the study of current events through the already mentioned approaches, the students will have sufficient background to investigate current events through the problems approach. A class discussion should lead to the listing of problems on the various news fronts. Such problems as desegregation, the United Nations, taxes, and disarmament will be suggested and committees can be organized to investigate those selected for study.

- *By Areal Study.* Extending this approach further is the areal study. Each of the study groups is given an area such as South America, Africa, or a specific region of our own country. At other times you may wish to feature specific countries. If, for instance, you are studying South America in social studies, you may wish to have committees watching for news about Brazil, Argentina, Chile, and so forth.

- *By Individual Topic.* Another approach within the same framework is the topical approach which studies science, art, music, education, as they occur in the news. In this way students keep up to date with happenings in various areas of study.

- *By Parts of the Newspaper.* If your purpose is also to study the make-up of the newspaper as a part of mass media, you may organize the study of current events around the different parts of the newspaper. Groups can report on editorials, the financial page, radio and TV, sports, feature writers and columnists.

It is recommended that you try various types of organization in order to avoid a monotonous routine which leads to boredom rather than interest.

► The press conference

Conduct a press conference in your room occasionally to arouse interest and lend variety to the study of current affairs. Students from the fourth grade and up will be pleased with this technique, particularly since the teacher actively participates. The teacher plays the role of a prominent individual (students are seldom sufficiently skilled or knowledgeable to play the role).

The teacher announces that the class will have a press conference with someone like the President of the United States, the governor of your state, an astronaut, a well-known author, or an international statesman. It is explained that, since the person named cannot be present on the specified day, the teacher will serve as a stand-in.

Planning and study on the part of both the interviewers and interviewee are necessary. Have students write sample questions so they can learn what constitutes a penetrating question. Assign reading in newspapers and other periodicals to facilitate intelligent participation in the conference.

The procedure follows that of press conferences which class members should observe on television. The interviewee enters the room (playing the role seriously), makes a short statement, and asks for questions, calling on various reporters in turn. The students act as reporters, asking pertinent questions about current problems.

After some practice a guest may be invited to be interviewed by the group. Perhaps a well-informed fellow-teacher will play a specific role or you may invite a city official to visit your classroom. (Be sure to explain the activity fully to him.)

This activity lends itself to correlation with the language arts. The reporters learn oral communication skills as they present their questions. They learn to take notes during the interview. After the interview they write copy for their newspaper, reporting the press conference. Their reports of an interview can be compared to see how different individuals handle the same material and also to check the accuracy of reporting.

The entire class will be involved in this activity as they become more news conscious. Conferences can be held periodically with the announcement made in advance so that students have ample time to prepare. Copies of current news magazines and newspapers, as well as access to the *Readers' Guide,* will facilitate their study of the activities of persons being featured. This activity can be prepared individually and hence can be challenging to students at all ability levels.

► Contemporary events scrapbook

The scrapbook of contemporary events is easily adaptable to any grade level. Its chief object is to train students to be more selective in their choice of news items. It can be carried out on a class basis or by a group. The scrapbook of current events generally contains the best (the most significant) news article brought in for any one day. This selection is made by a committee or by the class and pasted in the scrapbook with the date and source noted.

Once each week the pages of the scrapbook can be reviewed to determine the most significant stories for that week. You may wish to mark these stories in some way (a star, perhaps). At longer intervals of time the class should review the news events so marked. At the end of the semester the top ten stories that have been in the news may be selected.

This type of selection would lead to the discussion of the qualities of a newsworthy story. What makes news that is of some lasting significance? The quality of the writing of these stories can also be discussed. Students may then try to write news stories.

This study of contemporary events is very flexible as far as the time spent on the study, the number of students working on the activity, and the depth of the study are concerned. Students might, for example, work on these various levels of such an activity:

1. Collection of daily news articles mounted in a scrapbook.
2. The collection of articles with periodic evaluation.
3. Collection of articles, periodic evaluation, and selection of the ten best stories of the year.
4. Reorganization of collected articles into a book, *News of the Year.*

► People in the news

Much news revolves around famous figures on the contemporary scene—presidents, prime ministers, astronauts, authors, scientists. A good way for students to become familiar with the events of the day is to become familiar with the people connected with these events.

This idea may be initiated by a short discussion of men being studied in history. The students may then consider those people who are making history today. List the names of these people on the board as they are mentioned.

After a sufficient number have been listed, let each student select one person whom they will investigate. There are many ways that the individual student can find information about the person he has chosen to study:

1. Follow the news in magazines, newspapers, and on television and radio for current information.
2. Check *Readers' Guide to Periodical Literature* for articles about the person. (Available at the public library.)
3. Use encyclopedias, *Current Biography, Who's Who?* for biographical data.
4. Refer to card catalog for biographies, books written by the person.
5. Write a letter to the person.

After a set length of time (a month) the student should prepare his information for presentation to the class. This does not mean that all students will give a formal oral report, but all will compile the information in a book form which may be used as a reference tool by other members of the class. Bound in inexpensive pamphlet binders, these reports can be placed in the school library.

The books will, of course, be done at different levels of ability. Some able students will draw portraits, develop family trees, investigate related areas or events, draw caricatures and cartoons, make a diorama, write a short play, or draw pictures depicting events in the person's life. Some students who become engrossed in the study will continue the study individually. Interesting covers for the books as well as provocative titles can be developed. The current events bulletin board will continue to feature these people as they occur in the news.

▶ **The news in pictures**

Another way the news is portrayed is through the pictures included in the newspaper. Students are interested in the pictorial aspects of the news, and these pictures can be studied at different levels of development. Students bring in pictures from the newspaper with a group (acting as an Editorial Board) selecting the picture which best illustrates the most significant news item of the week. The picture can be of a person or an event. These pictures are then collected in a notebook, reviewed periodically, and made available for use by the class.

An interesting variation: Newspaper pictures can be used for reviewing current events. Students mount selected pictures of people, places, and events on stiff paper such as tagboard. On the back of each mounting have students print several lines of information regarding the significance of the picture. Regarding a person, for example, they might include the name, position, and reasons for the person's fame. For some events pictured the caption clipped from the newspaper may be mounted on the back. Primary children will be able to identify certain people, such as the president or a currently famous astronaut, but children in the upper grades will quickly learn to identify many people in the news.

• *The Black Box.* An interesting activity can be developed from this study of pictured news which will further motivate interest in current events. The class should be divided into two teams to play *The Black Box.* A leader, called "the Wizard," is selected to conduct the game and a scorekeeper is appointed.

Place mounted pictures of people in the news (pictures must be large enough to be seen by class) in a large box which has been appropriately painted. The first student on Team A is shown a picture from the box by the Wizard. The team member must identify the pictured person for one point and tell one significant fact about the person for an additional point. A time limit (2 minutes) should be set to keep the game moving.

If Team A's student cannot identify the figure presented, he loses his turn, and the picture is then presented to the first person on Team B. By identifying the figure and telling a significant fact about the person, this student can win two extra points for Team B. If, however, the first student on Team B cannot identify the figure either, he also loses his turn and wins no points. The Wizard then presents the picture to the whole class, asking, "Who knows this man (or woman)?" He chooses a person to give the correct answer. The Wizard then puts the picture at the bottom of the pile and presents the next picture to Team B's second player. (This is really Team B's first turn.) This activity can be used for short periods of time by any number of students. It might be conducted before school starts or at lunch time.

• *Testing for Current Events.* The picture also serves as an excellent test of knowledge about current events. Pictures can be mounted on a bulletin board with a number beneath each one. Each student numbers his paper and writes the name of the person or event depicted beside the appropriate number. You may wish to have the students write additional information regarding each picture included in the test explaining the significance of the picture as well as merely identifying it.

▶ Contemporary time line

An interesting device to focus student attention on events and people making current history is the contemporary time line. The construction of the time line sets events in sequence of time and helps to develop the students' concept of time.

A year or less should be the period of time depicted by the contemporary time line. In this way a larger scale can be used. A practical scale for this type of line is one or two inches to represent each day. If, for example, your class begins the line in January with the intent of continuing it until the end of the year, the finished mural will be about 15 feet long if one inch equals one day.

It would be wise to prepare the paper in separate pieces about 36 inches by 18 inches for each month. The students can prepare the time line for the first month, marking significant events as they occur. Newspaper clippings or student drawings may be pasted near the appropriate date as desired. The students should discuss what events are of sufficient significance to be shown on the time line.

When this month has passed and the line is completed, mount this portion of the time line in a place that can be easily seen. A good place is often on the wall above a chalkboard or bulletin board. The next portion of the time line is then prepared. Each portion is mounted after a month has passed until the time line is completed.

The time line should be viewed and reviewed periodically. It may be that students will discover that some significant event was excluded and should be added. It is also possible that at times they will find that an insignificant event was recorded which should be eliminated. The time line should be a working device which will add to the learning of the students. It is not merely an ornament.

2

UTILIZING
COMMUNITY RESOURCES

The main purposes of this chapter are: (1) to point out the possibilities and the riches available in the community, and (2) to point out means by which these riches may be mined by the teacher and her class. There are almost limitless possibilities available to the school in any community. There is no school that cannot find some community resources to assist in enriching its school program.

▶ Exploring the possibilities

Before the school can make use of community resources, it is necessary to know what is available. For this purpose many schools have developed a file of community resources. Files are sometimes developed by the following groups:

- Teachers' workshops
- Students in social studies classes
- Librarians (public, school, county)
- Parent-teacher committees
- School central office (audio-visual consultant)
- College or university facilities
- County school office

When deciding to develop a file for your individual school, question first the above groups to determine whether there is already a file in existence for your geographic area. In this way you will avoid needless duplication of effort. If you should find that one or more of the groups mentioned does maintain such a file, you then wish to examine the file to see if it meets your requirements. Several points you would want to examine would be: Is the file up to date, complete, available, and appropriate?

If there is no adequate file available to you, then one should be developed. One way to begin collecting information for this type of file is to develop one questionnaire to send to parents and another questionnaire to send to local industries and organizations.

A simple questionnaire, like the sample given below, can be sent to parents and other community members. The purpose of this questionnaire is simply to determine whether there are people who have information, skills, or talents to offer to the schools. This questionnaire also discovers whether there are various types of realia (objects, such as tools, costumes, etc., which help relate people's daily living to the classroom) which the school might borrow to enrich the study of, for example, a country.

SAMPLE QUESTIONNAIRE
COMMUNITY MEMBERS

Dear Patron:

Our school is studying the community to determine what resources are available to the school. Do you have some talent, skill, or information that you could share with us? If so, please fill out this form and return it to the school.

What is your speciality? (Hobbies, travels, pictures, and others)

_____

_____

_____

_____

_____

Your Name _____

Address _____

Phone _____

A second questionnaire should be constructed to be sent to local industries and organizations to determine what types of field trips are possible in your community. This questionnaire will also discover speakers, exhibits, films, etc., which might be useful to the school. A questionnaire like the one shown on page 14 might be used.

The distribution of this questionnaire will be through the mail, so addresses must be obtained. The yellow pages of the telephone book will yield many ideas for places that might be of interest and help to the school and will give the address and phone number. Typical agencies that usually appear in every telephone book are:

Airports, train stations

Airlines, railroad companies

Newspapers, TV and radio stations

Art Galleries, museums, libraries, zoos, observatories

United States government agencies (agriculture, forestry, military)

State government (police, parks, historical monuments, museums)

Local city government (fire, police, library, city buildings)

Industries (lumbering, steel mills, electronics)

Colleges, universities, specialized schools

Another source of addresses might be a nearby college or uni-

---

SAMPLE QUESTIONNAIRE
FIRMS AND ORGANIZATIONS

Dear Sir:

Our school is studying the community in an attempt to determine what types of study trips and resource people are available to the school. Would you please fill out the following information:

Name of firm or organization: _____

Nature or type of business or activity _____

Is your establishment open to visitors? _____

Address: _____

Briefly describe the activities, things to see: _____

_____

_____

_____

Name of contact person: _____

Telephone: _____

Is guide service available? _____

How many students can be accommodated? _____

What time of day is best for the trip? _____

How much advance notice is needed? _____

For what grade level is the trip recommended? _____

Other comments or information: _____

_____

_____

_____

_____

---

versity. They frequently maintain a speaker's bureau. Names of exchange students from foreign countries are available, too.

The local chamber of commerce or the local newspapers might be able to supply names and addresses of organizations such as Toastmasters, League of Women Voters, American Association of University Women, etc. These organizations might supply speakers, and they might also suggest other sources of information.

Let others know about your project, for other groups such as the P.T.A. or League of Women Voters might be interested in helping develop the file so that their organization might have access to its information. As you explore these sources, you will find that often one leads to another. The lists given here are not exhaustive, for any community will have distinctive resources.

After the questionnaires have been distributed and begin to return, the information obtained should be recorded on cards to start the file. This clerical task can be done by students, parents, or the school secretary. These cards should contain only essential information as in the sample shown here:

SUBJECT HEADING   Grade level_____

Name of firm or organization _____

Address _____

Activities, things to see _____

_____

_____

Name of contact person _____

            Telephone _____

Guide service? _____ Number of students _____

Time of day _____ Advance notice _____

Other comments and information _____

_____(Continue on back)

The card file should be organized according to the needs of the school which it serves. A functional type of organization for the school Resource File is by geographic area or topic of study. Examples of representative categories which are often included are:

Your city	Transportation
Your county	Africa
Your state	Mexico
Communication	

Different colored cards may be used for designating speakers, field trips, etc. If a source is applicable to more than one topic, cross-filing should be used.

When the file is ready for use, it is very important that it be placed where it can be easily used. The best location is sometimes the office, the library, but perhaps the most functional location is in the teachers' room, where the teachers can examine the file at their leisure.

A file of this sort must be kept up to date. It should be re-examined each year and constantly added to as new information is acquired. Information contained in the resource file should be publicized through bulletins, the teachers' bulletin board, special leaflets on "Trips to Take," flyers made available by organizations represented, or discussion at staff meetings.

It is a good idea to place a card at the front of the file containing general information on school policies regarding field trips, and the use of the source people. A number of blank permission slips can also be kept available in this file.

▶ Using the field trip most effectively

Once the file of community resources is developed, how should it be utilized? One of the most common and effective ways is the taking of a field trip to visit an industry or organization. In order to demonstrate the use of this technique let us plan a hypothetical field trip with Miss Fuller's fifth grade class, which is studying modes of transportation in the United States. Let us follow Miss Fuller's handling of the three parts of the field trip: (1) Pre-planning, (2) The Trip, and (3) The Follow-up.

• *Pre-planning.* Miss Fuller has decided that a field trip might be appropriate to clarify the students' knowledge about modes of transportation. Her first step is to check with the principal to determine the school policy regarding such trips. (Check on this when you first start teaching in a new school district.) She needs to know about available bus facilities, any time limit, and permission forms to be completed by parents.

Then Miss Fuller examines the section of the Resource File entitled TRANSPORTATION to discover what trips are most appropriate for her grade level and for her objectives. Let us suppose that a trip to Great Western Airlines is selected. The criteria she uses to select this trip are these:

1. Is it appropriate to the course of study?

2. Does it provide experience and knowledge for the students which could not be gained as well in another way?
3. Is it suitable for the children in the class?

• *Getting in Touch with the Contact.* After selecting this trip Miss Fuller telephones Mr. Spaulding, the contact person listed on the card. She has a list of questions she wants to ask at this time about the length of the trip, the tentative date she would like to visit the airlines, and the starting place for the trip. She also wants to know whether there are facilities for eating and if any materials are furnished to the teacher to aid pre-teaching.

The contact person at the airlines should be informed of the particular requirements of Miss Fuller's class, what the group wishes to accomplish on the trip, and the background of the class. The airline representative may also mention further requirements or recommendations. Miss Fuller may make arrangements, too, for going to the airport prior to the field trip to familiarize herself with the facilities.

Following her conversation with Mr. Spaulding of the airlines, Miss Fuller checks with her principal to reconfirm the date for the trip and to requisition the necessary transportation. She also obtains the required permission slips from the school secretary. (See the sample form.)

SAMPLE PERMISSION FORM

Dear Parents:

Our class is planning to visit _____
(Place)

_____ on _____.
(Date)

We will be gone from school from _____ to _____.
(Time)   (Time)

This study trip is an important part of our social studies program and will add to our learning about _____.

Please sign this form indicating your willingness to have your child participate in this learning activity.

Sincerely yours,

_____
(Teacher)

_____ has my permission to
(Child)

participate in a study trip under the supervision of the class teacher on

_____. Signed:_____
(Date)   (Parent)

The class now becomes involved in the planning of the trip. The objectives of the proposed trip are discussed and listed. The students fill out the necessary information on the permission slips which are then taken home for their parents' signatures. These slips should go home on Monday or Tuesday of the week before the trip is taken, which allows ample time for their return.

• *Briefing the Class.* The class can then discuss the necessity for setting standards of behavior on the bus and at the airport. If they are involved in developing these standards, they will be more inclined to follow them. It should be made clear that the trip is a learning activity taken during school hours and that the class members should act accordingly.

The route to be taken can be mapped ahead of time by the class. The teacher can inform the students of things they will see en route. If the trip is to be long, they can also plan suitable activities for the bus trip. Each member of the class should be given a duplicated copy of a simple map showing the route for the trip and the points of interest to be noted. Each student can then *follow the map as the trip is taken.*

Miss Fuller decides to use *the "buddy" system* to make certain no one gets lost on the trip. This system means that each student chooses a friend with whom to travel. It is understood that they are to be together at all times during the trip.

She also plans to use a hand signal which she has developed for use on the playground. She reviews this means of *getting attention* with the students so that all understand. When Miss Fuller raises her right hand high in the air, all students do likewise and stand quietly, so she can give directions.

The students, together with Miss Fuller, discuss what questions will be answered by the trip. They plan to take notes so that information will be accurate and complete.

• *The Trip.* The day of the trip arrives and the students prepare for the countdown:

5   All permission slips checked in.
4   Review of standards of behavior.
3   Review of purposes of trip and questions to be answered.
2   Check on clothing, lunches, money.
1   Last count of students.
0   Blast off—into the bus and away.

Miss Fuller will see that her students have adequate rest stops, that they are conforming to standards of behavior, and will periodically check on the presence of all students. The trip should, however, be a pleasant, enjoyable learning experience for the students and the teacher. Once the group arrives at the airport the guide provided will conduct the tour.

• *Follow-up.* The trip is not complete when the group arrives back in the classroom. The follow-up activities are as much a part of the trip as were the pre-planning activities. They must be carried out if the trip is to reap its fullest harvest.

The follow-up should begin with a discussion of what the students learned. How many questions were answered from the list compiled prior to the trip? A display can be made of the brochures, leaflets, and any realia gained from the trip. As part of the language arts, curriculum letters should be composed thanking the airlines officials for the opportunity of visiting the airport.

Miss Fuller will note her reactions to this trip on the card in the Resource File. The notes she makes may be helpful to another teacher when planning a like trip.

Students should discuss the behavior during the trip. Discussion will lead to suggestions for any future trips.

Every question answered by this field trip will suggest more questions to the students. The trip should serve to whet the students' interest in the subject. It may lead to further library research. It may also lead to the need for additional outside help in supplying specific information. This need may lead to the use of a resource person listed in the Resource File.

► *Supplementing your teaching efforts with guest speakers*

Miss Fuller discovers in checking the file under TRANSPORTATION again that the father of one of the sixth grade children is a pilot for one of the large airlines. He should be able to answer the many questions which particularly the boys have about flying.

• *Preparing the Guest.* She again checks with the principal on the procedure to be followed in having a guest speak to the class. She then calls Mr. Flagg, the pilot, to see whether he will be able to visit the class. They set a date for the visit and she gives him some information about the needs of the students and a brief explanation of their backgrounds. She also tells him that she would like him to speak about 30 minutes and allow for a 15-minute question period at the end.

Miss Fuller also suggests that Mr. Flagg wear his uniform since the students will be very much interested in seeing it. Mr. Flagg mentions that he plans to bring copies of maps used in flying and some models of present-day aircraft.

Miss Fuller thanks Mr. Flagg and tells him that two students will meet him in the office at 1 o'clock.

• *Briefing the Class*. Again, as with the field trip, the students discuss what questions they would like to have Mr. Flagg answer. This discussion helps to focus their thinking and may raise the level of questions asked of the visitor. The students should be prepared to take notes during the pilot's presentation.

Two students are chosen to serve as escorts for the guest; one student prepares to introduce Mr. Flagg to the class and to the teacher. A helpful technique, too, is to assign one student to thank the speaker at a signal from the teacher. This technique not only properly thanks the visitor but also serves to end the presentation when it is appropriate.

3

USING THE BULLETIN BOARD

The purpose of this chapter is to describe techniques for using display space which will aid the classroom teacher in making full use of this teaching technique. We will discuss (1) Ideas for Bulletin Boards, (2) Materials for the Display, (3) Improvising Display Space, and (4) Using Student Assistance.

▶ Ideas for bulletin boards

Where do you get an idea for an interesting bulletin board? This in itself stymies many teachers. There are a number of different sources of good ideas.

• *Class Work.* Class studies will lead naturally to many effective displays which will serve to reinforce learning or motivate interest. A common use of bulletin board space is for STAR PAPERS (papers of those students getting a perfect score on a social studies test are exhibited bearing the star seal).

After the class has returned from its field trip to the airport the students will want to display materials obtained during this trip. A bulletin board, OUR TRIP, will naturally develop including papers, brochures, and leaflets, while booklets and realia are placed on a table or shelf below.

You will find that the bulletin board can serve to present a test of information being studied. If the class has been studying the United States, you may display an outline map showing only the state boundaries (use the opaque projector to enlarge a small map). The caption, TESTING . . . 1, 2, 3, may be placed at the top of the space. As you point to each state, the student must write the name of the state and perhaps its capital. The map can be used as the students check the test to show the state when each is properly identified. The students can use this blank map to review the location of the states.

If you want to motivate interest in the study of, for example, California, try pinning up pictures and articles about this state a week before you wish to begin the study. Include a sizable map and pictures of scenes from California with an appropriate caption —HAVE YOU BEEN TO CALIFORNIA? or CALIFORNIA, HERE WE COME. Students will begin discussing the pictures, investigating the map, and will be ready to study this area in more detail.

• *Periodicals and Books.* A number of magazines feature bulletin board ideas regularly each month. You should check some of them for possible ideas that you can reproduce at least in part. Some magazines you will want to investigate include the following:

Wilson Library Bulletin, 950 University Avenue, New York 52, New York.
Instructor, Dansville, New York.
Grade Teacher, 28 Leroy Avenue, Darien, Connecticut.

Pamphlets and books are often written to help the teacher prepare effective displays. Check the card catalog to see what materials are listed under Displays, Bulletin Boards, or Exhibits. Comprehensive books on the use of audio-visual aids will contain a section on the use of the bulletin board and other display techniques. Listed here are several handbooks which are recommended:

Dent, Charles, and Ernest Tiemann, *Bulletin Boards for Teaching.* Austin, Texas: University of Texas Press, 1955.
Koskey, Thomas, *Baited Bulletin Boards.* San Francisco: Fearson, 1954.
Miller, Ray, *Bulletin Boards, High, Wide, and Handsome.* Riverside, California: Bruce Miller, 1957.
Ryan, Marion, *How to Use a Bulletin Board.* Washington, D.C.: National Council for the Social Studies, 1953.
Stolper, B. J. R., *The Bulletin Board as a Teaching Device.* New York: Columbia University Press, 1946.

• *Other Teachers.* One of the best sources of new ideas is the colleague who teaches down the hall. As you visit other classrooms, you will often get a new idea for creating an interesting display. It may be a Christmas idea which you can't use until next year, but file it away for future consideration.

• *The File of Bulletin Board Ideas.* You should start a file of bulletin board ideas. You can start this file at any time by simply buying a package of unlined 4x6 file cards. As you encounter each new idea for the bulletin board, make a quick sketch of it and file it away. Be on the lookout for catchy captions.

This file is particularly helpful when it comes to holidays such as Columbus Day, Lincoln's and Washington's birthday, Christmas, etc. It is also good for displays which teach concepts and serve as teaching aids.

Be sure to keep the sketches of the idea simple or the keeping of the file will become too time consuming to be practical. Organize the cards by topics, holidays, etc., as soon as you accumulate enough to make it necessary. A typical card is shown below.

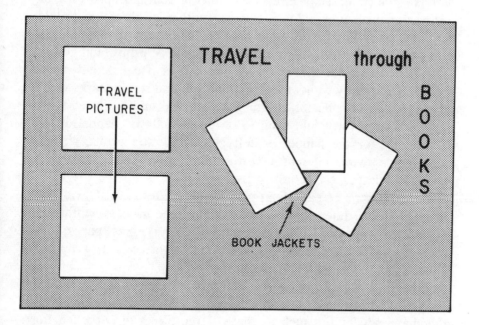

► *Materials for the display*

If you collect materials which are suitable for use in creating a display, you will soon find that constructing a bulletin board captioned, for example, YARNS ABOUT THE OLD WEST, which features stories of the westward movement, will be easy. You can quickly staple a burlap background to the corkboard, use a skein of contrasting yarn to "write" the caption (use pins to hold the letters in place), and scatter appropriate book jackets along a yarn which leads out from the caption and around the rest of the board. Let us consider some of the types of things you will need to collect as aids in preparing effective bulletin boards without undue effort.

• *Backgrounds.* Most bulletin boards are of cork or other neutral colored material, an acceptable background for certain displays. If used at all times, however, this background becomes dull and unnoticed. For this reason you will want to vary the backgrounds for your displays according to the color scheme and the type of display planned.

There are a number of background materials which can be quickly and easily attached to the display area. One of the simplest effective background materials is cloth. A worthwhile investment is the purchase of several yards of colored burlap. An inexpensive variety of burlap, usually available for less than 50 cents per yard, is about 40 inches wide and comes in a number of interesting colors. Pinned or stapled to the bulletin board, it provides an interesting background for pictures or other displayed materials.

There are a number of other types of cloth that are suitable for this purpose. Experiment with different textures, prints, and colors. The chief advantage of cloth over any sort of paper is that it can be used repeatedly without tearing, and pin and staple marks won't show. It can also be folded for easy storage and easily cleaned. Types of cloth you might want to try are as follows: flannel or felt (especially for the flannel or felt board); cotton prints, stripes, solid colors with different textures; netting; discarded materials (curtains, drapes, tablecloths, spreads).

Different sorts of paper can also be used effectively if available in large sheets. Interesting papers which come in wide widths are as follows: wallpaper (different textures, colors); grass paper; corrugated cardboard (large rolls of varied bright colors); wrapping paper (foil, tissue, figured); rice paper.

Other unusual effects can be obtained by experimenting with a variety of background materials. Keep your eyes open for materials that have possibilities such as these: large pieces of cork; fencing (chicken wire, other wire varieties); bamboo drapes (matchstick, split); screening.

• *Lettering.* The lettering on a display is perhaps one of the most important elements as it must catch the eye and the interest. It must, therefore, be *easily read* at a distance. For this reason avoid fancy script which is hard to make, hard to read.

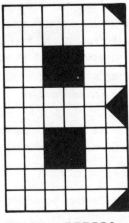

BLOCK LETTERS

In the lower grades use manuscript printing which the students are accustomed to reading. Later a simple block letter may be used. The students in the upper grades can assist you in constructing several stiff paper alphabets of different colors in a standard size. These alphabets can be used a number of times before some letters must be replaced. Construct patterns on squared paper (four squares to one inch) as shown left. Some

24

schools find it convenient to purchase sets of white plastic or cardboard letters. These letters are attractive and easy to use if enough are purchased so that each teacher has her own or if teachers return those not in use to a central location. Do avoid purchasing those varieties which are expensive and highly breakable. You may wish to send for catalogs from these companies:

Artype, Inc., 549 West Randolph Street, Chicago, Illinois.
Cello-Tak Lettering Corp., 131 West 45th Street, New York 36, New York.
Redi-Kut Letter Co., 185 North Prairie, Hawthorne, California.

An invaluable aid in making captions quickly is the felt pen, which comes in varied colors of ink. If you keep on hand a quantity of strips of white drawing paper or tagboard, you can print the words needed for a bulletin board rapidly, pinning the strips directly on the display. These pens can be purchased at local stationers or from manufacturers such as these:

Dri-Flo Pen Co., 716 Junction Avenue, Detroit 9, Michigan.
Speedry Products, Inc., Richmond Hill 18, New York.

Occasionally experiment with other types of lettering for variation and interest. Here are some ideas you might like to try.

Write a short caption with heavy yarn, string, or rope.

YARNS OF THE WEST   CORRAL THESE BOOKS

Cut large black letters from newspaper (may be pasted on heavier paper which is allowed to extend, forming, for example, a red outline for each letter).

WHAT'S NEW?   NEWS VIEWS

Hang stiff paper letters on the end of pins to give a three-dimensional effect. (Feature an owl figure for the first; pictures of historical events, dates, for the second.)

WHO KNOWS?   WHAT HAPPENED WHEN?

• *The Picture File*. One of the most important types of material used in creating an effective bulletin board is the picture. It is important, therefore, that you collect good pictures either as an individual or as a school. The development of a comprehensive Picture File is a worthwhile project for a teachers' workshop or for a group of students. If teachers will pool their resources, an excellent file of pictures can be kept in a central place to which all teachers have access.

Usually pictures will fit inside a standard sized folder which can be labeled according to subject areas and topics. Some common topics often used include the following: Animals; Arctic Lands;

Birds; Book Jackets; Desert Lands; Flowers; France; Geology; India; Indians (American); Israel; Library; New England; New York City; Pacific Northwest; Sea Life. The headings suggested here are only a few of those that will be needed. Several teachers should make a list of the headings desired. The categories chosen will vary from grade to grade and according to the areas studied.

We do not recommend that all pictures clipped from magazines and other sources be mounted because of the time consumed by this additional task and the fact that mountings take up much room in the file as well as extra money for their purchase. If you do choose to mount some of the better pictures, choose one neutral color on which to mount all of these pictures. Never permanently mount some on red, others on blue, and so forth, as this limits the pictures' usefulness.

The Picture File will care for those pictures under 9x12, but other arrangements must be made for the larger pictures. As it is not desirable to fold any picture, the best facility is the large picture drawer which stores flat pictures. A notation should be made in the Picture File to indicate that a large picture is also available.

• *Sources of Pictures.* What are some of the sources of pictures of educational value? The first source one usually thinks of is the magazine. Let parents know that the school is developing a picture file. They can supply you with useful back issues of *Life, Holiday, National Geographic, Look,* and others. A one-year subscription to *Ideals* will provide the file with some fine seasonal pictures. *Arizona Highways* contains excellent pictures of that geographic area.

REMEMBER: When you or students clip pictures from magazines, check to see if the picture goes with a useful article which should also be kept for its information. This is especially true of *National Geographic.*

Another source of good pictures is the agency supplying free educational materials. Chapter 7 lists many names and addresses of organizations that will send schools informational material. The material sent often includes travel posters and pictures.

The school may have a fund which can be spent on purchasing commercial pictures. Pictures of the presidents, art prints, a paperbound copy of *The Family of Man* (New York: Pocket Books), *Ideals* (3510 W. St. Paul Avenue, Milwaukee 1, Wisconsin), are available at low cost. Books to be discarded should always be checked for pictures.

Other sources of pictures which can be collected are: newspapers (foreign, Sunday sections); calendars (interesting one by

26

Japan Air Lines, $1.50 from C. E. Tuttle, Rutland, Vermont); Christmas cards (look for UNICEF, art museum reproductions, e.g., New York City's Metropolitan Museum of Art); catalogs.

Listed here are several addresses of commercial suppliers of pictures which might be helpful in beginning a Picture File:

> Besler Visual Products Company, Inc.
> 210 East 23rd Street
> New York, New York

> Metropolitan Museum of Art
> Fifth Avenue and 82nd Street
> New York, New York

> Museum of Modern Art
> 11 West 53rd Street
> New York, New York

> Perry Pictures
> Box 4
> Malden, Massachusetts

• *Three-Dimensional Materials.* Besides pictures there are many other types of materials which can be displayed to lend interest in the topic being studied. Include some realia even on the bulletin board. An item of clothing from a foreign country can be pinned on the board, lending a three-dimensional effect to the display. A lightweight model plane can be incorporated in a bulletin board about transportation by fastening the model with string, which is tacked to the board. This display might be captioned I C U R TAKING A TRIP (I See You Are Taking a Trip) and feature a large eye drawn by a student.

Heavier models, books, dolls dressed in native costume, and other related materials may be exhibited on a table in front of the bulletin board. Yarn or ribbon may lead from the item displayed to a map on the board above.

A useful type of sign which stands securely can be made for the table exhibit. Fold a 9x12 (or larger) piece of construction paper into thirds lengthwise. On the center section print the word that fits the exhibit. Then form the folded paper into an elongated triangle and hold it in place with pieces of transparent tape. This sign can be seen at a distance.

To lend interest to any display use paper sculpture for the three-dimensional effect. Some paper sculpture is simple, while other ideas require hours of work. Your use of this technique will depend on how much time you want to spend on it. Let your students experiment with making some of the fascinating ideas described in the books listed here:

Johnson, Pauline, *Creating with Paper*. Seattle: University of Washington Press, 1958.
Johnston, Mary G., *Paper Shapes and Sculpture for School Use*. Worcester, Massachusetts: Davis Publications, Inc., 1958.
Murray, William D. and Francis J. Rigney, *Paper Folding*. New York: Dover, 1960.
Origami; Japanese Paper Folding. Tokyo: Toto Shuppan Co., Ltd., 1957. Distributed by Japan Publications Trading Co., Ltd., Box 722, Tokyo, Japan.

▶ *Improvising display space*

Usually a classroom will have at least one medium-sized cork bulletin board plus one or two chalkboards. This does not provide much space for displaying work of the students, for adding to the appreciation of art, or for motivating the students' interest in subjects like the social studies. More fortunate teachers may have one whole wall covered with cork as well as additional small boards, and yet they still wish they had more space.

• *Cork and Beaver Board.* If your room lacks sufficient space for display, you may need to improvise additional bulletin board space. The most obvious method to obtain more surface area is to cover unused wall space with cork. If the use of cork is prohibited, substitute a wallboard such as beaver board which can be painted or left the neutral color.

If there is no wall area free to create more bulletin board area, pieces of beaver board may be cut to fit a chalkboard and hung in place. They should be fitted so they can be removed and set aside if the chalkboard is to be used.

• *Easel Boards.* Large easel display boards can be constructed from two pieces of wallboard joined by hinges at the top. A strip of wood holds the two boards open when in use. Remove the strip of wood and the boards fold together for storage.

• *Bamboo Hangings.* Bamboo hangings made from discarded bamboo curtains make interesting display areas. Pictures and other materials can be attached to the bamboo with pins set at angles. Other cloth hangings can be used in the same way.

• *Yarn and Wire.* Pictures can be attached to a yarn or wire in

28

the fashion of a clothesline art show. Clip-style clothespins hold pictures firmly while they are drying or being exhibited.

• *Wall.* Some pictures can be hung directly on the wall. Use masking tape which can be pressed against the back of the picture and circled around to press against the wall also. Commercial preparations of special bulletin board wax are used for this purpose also. The wax can be used repeatedly; the tape will not support anything very heavy nor can it be used a second time. This wax can be purchased from: Demco Library Supplies, Madison 1, Wisconsin, or New Haven 2, Connecticut.

• *Table tops, tops of book shelves, wide window sills.* All add space for displays. Realia can be placed here so students can view the articles more closely. Pictures can also be displayed flat or hung from the edge of a table or shelf.

• *Charts.* Charts mounted on stiff cardboard provide additional display material. These charts have the advantage that they can stand in the chalk tray not requiring bulletin board space. They can also be used repeatedly just as they are, without necessitating the preparation of a display.

• *Mobiles.* Some types of material may be displayed in the unique style of the mobile. Puppets made by the class might be hung from ribbons for an Open House exhibit of the students' work. Unbreakable, lightweight realia might also be effectively displayed in this fashion.

▶ Using student assistance

It is impossible for the busy teacher to change bulletin boards as frequently as necessary and to prepare materials for new ones without some help from her students. Students enjoy assisting the teacher and learn much about arranging a display as they participate. They will also gain information as they handle the pictures, articles, realia, and other items to be displayed.

• *Organize a Committee.* A bulletin board committee should be established. Children on this committee may or may not have artistic talent as there is much more than drawing involved. Although you will wish to rotate positions on such a committee, it is best to have students serve for perhaps a month so that they will actually learn the techniques. Also it is wise not to replace the whole committee at one time. If the committee contains six members, replace only two at a time so that new members can learn from experienced members.

This committee can work on making sets of letters as needed.

They can also help check magazines for appropriate pictures, clipping them carefully according to your instructions. Short periods of instruction will avoid careless work by these committee members. General points that students will need to be taught include the following:

- Captions are like titles. They should be short and provocative.

  TRAVEL TIPS

  PUPIL PUZZLERS

  LET'S TALK TURKEY

  1492 (or any other significant date)

- It is best not to display too much at any one time. A simple display is more effective than a cluttered one.

- Plan the display on a sheet of paper; then lay the material on a table so that you can check it before it is mounted on the bulletin board.

- Contrast is important. Light colors and dark colors used in contrast are effective.

- Colors chosen to be used together should be pleasant.

- The display should be balanced, but never divide the area exactly in half.

4

CHALLENGING
THE GIFTED STUDENT

Described in this chapter are three activities especially suitable for the gifted student: (1) The Area Study, (2) The Contemporary Newspaper, and (3) Dear Diary. . . . Within the first weeks of school you will notice those students who appear to be outstanding. They probably have above average IQ scores, are excellent readers, contribute to class discussion, and have past records of high achievement. It is this group of perhaps three to five students who will benefit from an interesting activity which they can develop independently after they have completed other work.

Meet with this group of students while the rest of the class is busy with an assignment. Discuss with them the sorts of activities you would like to have them explore. The group may be organized as a club such as The Explorers' Club or The Researchers. The students may suggest other activities suitable for their group. It may be that they will have more suggestions after working on one of the activities described in this chapter.

After discussing possibilities for this group, the students may wish to wait a day before deciding on the first type of activity. This will give them an opportunity to think about the possible projects. Being involved in the selection of the specific project will lead to greater enthusiasm and interest in developing the project.

These social studies activities may be done individually or the group of gifted students may serve as a committee conducting one large study (as in the construction of the Contemporary Newspaper, described later). A group of students working together as a committee will learn the techniques of committee work while gaining factual knowledge about the subject studied.

A table or special shelf should be set aside for the storing of books, magazines, and art supplies which these students are using. During their free time they can go to the table or bring their materials to their own desks to work.

31

▶ The area study

Are you studying the United States this year? An interesting project for your gifted students is the Area Study. Such a study consists of collecting as complete information as possible about one geographic area such as a state, a city, a country, or a section of a country. All aspects of the area are explored—geography, history, government, people, economy, and so forth.

This project should not be extended over too long a period of time as pupils may lose their enthusiasm. A period from one month to six weeks is long enough. You may wish to establish a deadline ahead of time or the group of students can decide (after working on the project a week or two) about how much time they should plan to use.

STEP ONE:

Meet with the group of students to discuss the following: the type of project and the sort of information to be found; the sources of this information; keeping a reading record; note-taking; and the selection of an area by each student.

• *The Information to Be Found.* First describe the Area Study to the students. Talk about the sort of general information each will be searching for. Examples are size, population, date of entry into the United States, the flag, industries, places of interest, and historical events. The students will supply additional suggestions. Others will occur as the project develops. Each student should note these suggestions to help him as he begins exploring his own area.

• *Sources of Information.* Ask the students where they might find information such as that noted. Have them make a list of possible sources of information. A student who chooses, for example, to study our 49th state, Alaska, might gain information in some of the following ways:

1. Read books. For example:

> Non-fiction: Pilgrim, Mariette, *Alaska; Its History, Resources, Geography, and Government.* Caldwell, Idaho: Caxton, 1952.
>
> Fiction: Anauta (Eskimo woman), *Wild Like the Foxes.* New York: John Day, 1956.

2. Write for information:

Chamber of Commerce	Senator for Alaska	Division of Tourism
Anchorage, Alaska	Senate Building	Alaska Office Bldg.
(or other cities)	Washington, D.C.	Juneau, Alaska

3. Obtain copies of newspapers and magazines:

> Anchorage *Daily Times;* Anchorage *Daily News; Alaska Sportsman* (Box 1271, Juneau, Alaska), sold at many magazine counters.

4. Check *Readers' Guide* for magazine articles about Alaska.
5. Begin a clipping file of pictures and articles.
6. Talk to people who have visited the country.
7. Study almanacs, atlases, encyclopedias for statistics.
8. Obtain a pen pal in Alaska. (Send request to a city school district.)

REMINDERS:

Students should realize the importance of developing research skills. Keeping a record of the sources of their information, for example, enables them to prove their statements and helps them find the source again if they need to check information. Establishing an acceptable form for keeping this information is good training for later research. Maintain high standards of accuracy; students will quickly acquire the skill.

• *Keeping a Reading Record.* At this first organizational meeting discuss the keeping of a record of material read. This information will later be used in constructing the bibliography for the completed study. For each source of information a 3x5 card (or slip of paper) should be used to record the following:

Book or Pamphlet
> Author (last name first). *Title of Book.*
> Publisher, year of copyright. Pages read.
>
> *Example:* Coombs, Charles I. *Bush Flying in Alaska.*
> Morrow, 1961. Pages 99-121.

Magazine or Newspaper Article
> Author (last name first). Title of Article.
> *Magazine Name.* Date of Magazine. Pages read.
>
> *Example:* Spencer, Dave. "The Alaskan Moose." *The Alaska Sportsman.* May, 1962. Pages 14-16.

Encyclopedia Article
> *Name of Encyclopedia.* Title of Article.
> Volume. Pages read.
>
> *Example: Encyclopedia Britannica.* "Alaska."
> Volume I. Pages 498-506.

• *Note-Taking.* It is important that students learn early to take notes rather than copy endless pages of meaningless material. Although you cannot suddenly teach the students every skill they need, it would be wise to stress immediately several general points regarding note-taking. The class may study this skill or you can give this group of students further instruction later. Stress the following:

1. Don't just copy an article from an encyclopedia.
2. Notes are brief. They are not necessarily written in sentences. Only the essential information is written.
3. When taking notes, *first* record the source of the information

33

on the same sheet on which the notes will be written. Also make a bibliography card.

• *Selection of Areas.* Let each student select a specific geographic area for study. It is best if each person chooses a different area. Each is then ready to begin exploring, searching for information.

Basic reference tools should be available in an elementary school library. Those which are not available in your school may be found in the public library. Students should read both fiction and non-fiction in addition to using reference books.

Encourage students also to share their resources. One student may, for example, supply an interesting book about California which will help the person who has chosen to study that state. There will be little sense of competition with this project as each tries to find complete information about his own area.

STEP TWO:

Another brief meeting should be held two or three days after the first one. The student will have begun explorations in finding material and information and will have been thinking about his project. He will also have taken some notes and written bibliography cards.

The main objects of this meeting are: (1) to answer questions, (2) to examine the reading record cards for the bibliography, and (3) to give the students more guidance in note-taking.

• *Questions.* Take a few minutes to answer any general questions which the students may have regarding their first efforts at finding information. An answer to one student's question may help the other students.

• *Bibliography Cards.* Ask to see the bibliography cards. Examine them with the group, explaining any errors made. If one student has made errors, others may need help along the same line.

It will be interesting, too, to note the types of sources they have used. Commenting on any unusual ones will be helpful to those who have not yet thought of that particular source. Again stress the desirability of sharing information. You may also suggest several additional books they may wish to examine.

• *Note-Taking.* (If the class is studying this technique, this section can be omitted at this time.) Give the students a duplicated sheet of factual material or select paragraphs from the social studies text. Ask the students to read the first group of paragraphs and to take notes as they read. Ask one student to write his notes on the board. Examine the notes of this student, making suggestions where necessary and pointing out the good features of his note-taking.

Repeat this procedure with another group of paragraphs so that all students working on the Area Study understand how to take notes. You may need to repeat this exercise if the students need more help.

STEP THREE:

Hold additional conferences when they seem necessary. At times you may find it satisfactory to talk individually to the students to determine how they are progressing. In this way you can give specific help as needed.

Some of the types of materials you may expect the researchers to include in the Area Study are listed here:

- Charts, graphs, diagrams showing factual information.
- Pictures drawn by the student depicting historical events, and so forth.
- Creative stories or poems about people, places, events.
- Mounted clippings from newspapers or magazines.
- Maps: Commercial road maps; drawn product, rainfall, historical maps.
- A time line for the area.
- Biographies of people from that area (brief).
- Brochures obtained from chambers of commerce, and so forth.
- Letters from people living in the area.
- Snapshots, postal cards, other pictures.
- Journalistic reporting of information.

Let the students think of as many types of things as they can. If, however, they come to a standstill, then suggest other types of material they might prepare, other avenues of exploration. They should prepare a variety of materials.

STEP FOUR:

The completed Area Study should include information, charts, and pictures prepared on sheets of the same size so that a book can be compiled. Similar materials should be grouped together.

Each student can prepare a table of contents, a title page, and a decorative cover. The bibliography should be included at the end of the book. The completed books are then presented to the class.

Each student may prepare a brief oral report, telling several interesting items about the state studied. He may want to show several charts or pictures as he reports to the class. Class members can then use the books as references.

▶ The contemporary newspaper

Are you planning to study the colonization of America, the Civil War period, or the settlement of the West this year? Let your group of bright students construct a Contemporary Newspaper suitable to the time in history being studied.

The Contemporary Newspaper is a newspaper constructed to resemble one printed at a given time in history. If your class is studying the Civil War, this newspaper might, for example, report the latest battle between the Blues and the Grays or the speech made by the President at Gettysburg. Advertisements, editorials, and pictures must be in keeping with the period.

Preparing one issue of an authentic paper will take the students from three to four weeks. It provides an excellent activity for gifted students. Often they become so engrossed in the project that they read widely at home or at the public library as well as at school.

STEP ONE:

At this first meeting you will need to explain the project and discuss the need for background information.

• *Explanation.* Explain the meaning of a Contemporary Newspaper. Perhaps some of the students have seen replicas or other student-made papers. Point out the fact that the class is, for example, now studying the Civil War, so that the paper would be an issue published during that time. Do not set a specific date yet, however, as that should come after more reading.

• *Background Information.* Students will probably want to start printing the newspaper immediately. You will need to stress the necessity for first obtaining more information, which they can get through reading, examining newspapers, and asking questions. Types of information they should begin finding include these: famous people who lived at this time; newsworthy events; what newspapers were like at this time; how people lived.

Discuss also the need for taking notes (see the description under the Area Study) and for keeping reading records on cards or slips of paper. All students require general background information. They may spend a week reading supplementary material about this period of history assuming that the entire class has already begun studying this period and is continuing its study.

The reading should include non-fiction such as the American Heritage Junior Library series, as well as biography such as Constance Burnett's *Captain John Ericsson, Father of the "Monitor,"* and fiction, for example, Enid Meadowcroft's *By Secret Railway.* If your school library does not have sufficient books on your subject, you can borrow books from the public library. Keep these reading materials on a table set aside for this purpose. Other students in the class may use these same materials for reports.

36

Having gained a little more information about the period, the students are now ready to consider the actual construction of a newspaper. At this meeting they will need to decide the definite date for their issue, choose positions on the newspaper staff, decide what is to be in the newspaper, and plan their work for the next week.

• *Date of the Issue.* Students will suggest interesting dates for the issue of the paper. Perhaps in the case mentioned, a date following a crucial battle may be selected, or they may choose to report Lincoln's Gettysburg Address given November 19, 1863, or his assassination in 1865.

• *The Newspaper Staff.* Discuss the various positions on a newspaper—editor, reporter, advertising manager, art editor—which will probably be enough to give each person a responsible position in the actual construction of the paper. Each student should have a part in writing some part of the paper; otherwise, he will not be busy at this time. Later jobs will involve printing and distributing.

The students may volunteer for these positions. The editor serves as chairman of the committee and with the teacher's assistance can conduct further conferences or meetings. Each student may need to do additional research regarding, for instance, advertising in a newspaper at this time.

• *Contents of the Paper.* The staff will have to decide what type of issue they will publish. One large newspaper can be constructed or small papers may be duplicated for class distribution. The large newspaper may be more authentic in appearance; also, more pages can be included than would usually be in a duplicated paper. Original pictures will be clearer, too, than those that are duplicated. There is also the problem of typing ditto masters or stencils if the paper is to be duplicated.

These problems should be carefully considered before deciding because it may make a difference in what types of material are used and how much can be included. Perhaps a facsimile of the front page alone could be prepared for duplication and distribution to the class, while the full paper is displayed for individual examination.

• *Gathering the News.* Students will then work individually on their part of the news coverage. They may have to do some more specific research to accomplish their assignments.

In order to publish the paper each student reporter is required to have his "copy" submitted by a certain deadline, so the paper can go to press. Printing may be done by a typist, if one of the students types (the teacher should *not* do it); otherwise it can be printed by hand. Headlines can be printed with a felt pen. Articles should be made to fit into the column spaces.

Stories and pictures should be laid on sheets of newsprint to determine the final spacing; articles may be prepared on pieces of typing paper or composition paper which are pasted to the newsprint or they may be printed directly on the newsprint. The latter process will show through on the other side if ink is used.

The completed paper should be presented to the class. Each participant in the project can tell briefly about an article or a problem involved in constructing the paper. The paper can then be laid on a table or mounted on the bulletin board so that other class members can read it.

▶ Dear diary . . .

Another interesting learning activity for gifted students is to pretend that they are famous historical figures. The student then keeps a diary describing his thoughts, his difficulties, his life through each day for a period of time. If the class is studying the discovery of America, for example, a natural choice would be Christopher Columbus, with the diary beginning perhaps on January 1, 1491. As Columbus, the student might begin the first entry in the diary thus: "I saw Juan Gonzalez today. I tried to tell him about my idea that the world is round, but he says I'm crazy. Maybe he's right. I get so discouraged. . . ."

Encourage the students to be creative in their presentation of these personalities. They should read to find out about the families, the friends, the things these people did other than the discovery for which they are chiefly known. In this way the people become more real for the students who can share and understand to some extent the problems these people faced.

Columbus might, for example, write on another day, "My wife is usually so understanding, but today she was feeling bad. She shouted and cried so all the neighbors heard her telling me that the children need food. She said I should look for a job . . ."

Later when he gets the support of King Ferdinand and Queen Isabella the diary would record the trials of getting the ships built, the lists of supplies, the actual voyage and its difficulties. There need not be an entry for each day as this might be too tedious.

Space should be allowed for days when something really crucial happens, as when the Queen tells Columbus she will help him.

STEP ONE:

The purpose of the first meeting is to describe the activity, let the students choose the person they want to study, and discuss the necessity for preliminary reading.

• *Describing the Activity.* Describe the proposed project to the students. Talk about the sorts of things people write in diaries. Ask if any of them have ever kept a diary.

• *Choosing a Person.* Have the students suggest names of well-known people connected with the present social studies unit. One student might write these on the chalkboard or a sheet of paper, so that the students may then select one person from the list. Each student should select a different person.

• *Preliminary Reading.* After each student has selected one person to study, suggest sources of information about famous people. The most helpful tool in this case will probably be the library's card catalog. Each student will want to read from more than one biographical account, as well as parts of books and articles in magazines. Again, each one should continue keeping a record of reading done. The students should also be acquiring skill in note-taking.

STEP TWO:

Meet with each student individually to check on his progress. Discuss his reading while examining the cards he is keeping to record his reading. Suggest other sources if necessary. Read also some of the entries he is writing for the diary. Suggest possible improvements.

STEP THREE:

For easy organization of the diary it is best to use a looseleaf notebook to hold the entries. Keeping entries on single sheets of paper which can be rearranged and altered freely allows more flexibility. If a student uses a spiral notebook, the entries follow compactly leaving no room for adding material to an entry that was made earlier. Often new information will give the student an idea for changing an earlier entry.

When the diary is completed, it can be presented to the class. The author might introduce his work in this fashion: "Researchers have just come across a fabulous discovery—a diary kept by Columbus in 1491 and 1492. This find sheds new light on the life of this man . . ." The student might then read several "significant" passages.

5

CORRELATING WITH OTHER SUBJECTS

Do you find it difficult to correlate subjects in today's busy curriculum? Let's explore the possibilities for correlating the social studies with language arts, art, and music.

If, for example, the class is studying France, it would be most appropriate then to use the music period to learn *Frère Jacques* or *Au Clair de la Lune.* These songs would not only teach music skills but would also further the students' understanding of the French people and their culture.

In the same way you might be drawing product maps of France which would teach map reading skills, increase knowledge about the products we get from France, and yet might also be the art lesson as the students draw pictures of various products and color the map attractively. Consider, too, the reading necessary to determine what the products of France are and in what part of France they are produced. The use of this unit method of study has many advantages.

It is a very flexible method. By adding music, art, reading, or language time to that allowed for social studies, the class can work in bigger blocks of time. The class may be busy writing biographies of famous French men or women, drawing pictures to accompany their presentations, reading to gather information, and making attractive book covers as they compile the finished product. Highly motivated and engrossed in the work at hand, they do not have to stop abruptly, put away their social studies work because it is suddenly time for language arts.

It is not being suggested that all subjects be connected to the social studies unit or that you use this method at all times. A lesson in arithmetic might really have to be contrived to fit into the French unit. When you are studying statistical information about this country, you might, however, also be practicing the reading of large numbers and the interpretation of graphs and charts. The students might be constructing graphs depicting various facts about population, production, and so forth. There continues to be a need for formal lessons in other subject areas when students need to learn specific skills.

• *Source Material.* Correlating the various areas of the curriculum requires pre-planning on the part of the teacher. Resource units listing books and materials and suggesting activities to enrich the analysis of one particular study area are often available commercially or are developed by school districts for their teachers' use. Two commercial sources are listed here:

The Instructor. Dansville, New York
Grade Teacher. 23 Leroy Avenue, Darien, Connecticut

At other times you may wish to develop a learning unit yourself. The library will provide assistance in finding materials for the unit to be developed. Here are some tools that will be helpful:

Readers' Guide to Periodical Literature
The Children's Catalog
The Standard Catalog for High School Libraries
Vertical file (pictures, articles, pamphlets)
Catalogs of free and inexpensive materials (See Chapter 7)

Described in the pages following are several activities which lend themselves to the correlation of several areas of the social studies curriculum. They are practical ideas which can be easily executed by any teacher. These are: the puppet show, art for world friendship, and the traveling classroom.

► The puppet show

The puppet show is an excellent means of correlating art, music, and the language arts with social studies. It is particularly good because it is a suitable activity for the entire class. Everyone can take part working at his level of ability. Often shy children will enjoy speaking through a puppet.

Everyone in the room then will make a puppet, and each student will also help write and produce a play. The class needs to decide first of all what sort of people, scenes, or animals it wishes to portray in puppetry. Working with the study of France, it might decide to have groups portraying the following:

A French fairy tale.
An original story set in Paris.
A story of real people in Brittany.
A biographical sketch of a famous French person—Marie Antoinette, Madame Curie, Napoleon, de Gaulle.

Students can then choose a topic. Each committee will discuss the story and decide on the characters to be included in their play. Some reading will have to be done to assure familiarity with the material to be presented. Then the play is written in dialogue form with a role for each member of the committee. The teacher should check to see that each student has a significant part in one of the plays.

After the play has been organized sufficiently, let each student choose one character for which to make a puppet. There are any number of different types of puppets which can be made, depending on the ages of the students, the degree of simplicity desired, and the time allotted for the study. Two types of puppets you may wish to try are: the stick puppet, which can be made and used on the same day; the hand puppet, which requires a little more time and skill.

• *Stick Puppets.* A simple puppet recommended for the primary grades is the stick puppet, constructed from materials which are readily accessible. Sticks from ice cream bars can be used or other thin flat sticks like tongue depressors. The tongue depressor is especially good, being wider and longer than the ice cream stick.

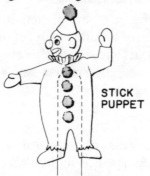

STICK PUPPET

To this stick is glued a figure drawn on stiff paper by the child; or figures cut from magazines and catalogs may be mounted on stiff paper and glued to the stick. Figures used must be large enough to be seen by the children at the back of the room during the puppet show.

In producing a puppet show younger children should depend on knowing the dialogue and action so that no reading is involved during the show. Children should not memorize long speeches, but depend on knowing the content of the speech. The production of this type of play should never be permitted to consume an undue amount of class time or become laborious with the student's striving toward professional perfection. The object of producing the puppet show is to promote the learning of concepts and information in the social studies. This objective must be kept in mind.

• *Hand Puppets.* Students in the intermediate grades will be interested in making various types of hand puppets. A practical type of lightweight puppet head that can be made in the classroom is that constructed of papier-mâché.

42

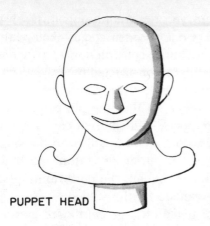

PUPPET HEAD

To retain the hole for the neck, work over a piece of dowel rod, rolled newspaper, or small cardboard tubing. Crushed newspaper can be tied in place to pad this core to obtain the approximate size and shape. Then apply one-inch strips of newspaper which have been dipped in a thick wheat paste solution (follow directions on the package for mixing).

After a few layers of newspaper have been applied, the features, ears, and shape of the face can be developed. If an animal puppet is being made, the shape of the animal's head will have to be considered carefully. A neck should be included with a protruding ridge at the bottom to hold the costume securely around the neck. To obtain a smooth finish apply a last layer of pink or white tissue paper, pasting it on and molding it to the desired features. The head is then ready to dry.

Hands are fashioned from newspaper strips and paste in the same way, molded over a small wire frame or folded newspaper. Again a ridge at the edge will hold the sleeve securely.

When thoroughly dry (allow two days), the head and hands are painted with water colors. A wig is made of yarn, fur scraps, or strips of cloth. Imagination will lead to many interesting finishing touches such as eyelashes.

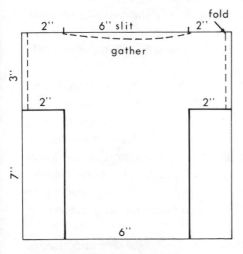

PUPPET COSTUME

The costume should be kept simple. The kimono style is easy for students to sew by hand. The basic kimono is cut from a suitable print and gathered at the neck and wrists as indicated in the diagram. Decorations can then be added. For women characters you may wish to add jewelry, an apron, a hat, or trimming around the bottom of the skirt. Men may be given a loose-fitting belt, a neckerchief, a cap, or a braid outline of trousers.

• *The Puppet Stage.* What can you use for a puppet stage? If your school does not own at least one wooden stage, explore the possibilities of getting one. It is a simple construction of plywood with hinged wings which can quickly be constructed by a woodshop in the junior or senior high school or by a willing parent.

The platform must be high enough so that the puppeteers are concealed while operating their puppets. Tall children can sit while short children may need a sturdy wooden box to adjust to the stage height. Draw curtains can be made of burlap or cotton and hung on a wire. A wire stretched six inches behind the performing platform can hold painted backdrops made by the students.

Temporary stages can be constructed of large cardboard cartons similar to a wooden stage. If the box available is not tall enough, place it on a table while in use. Children can also operate their puppets behind a table or desk using the writing surface as the stage platform.

The children will enjoy producing their plays for their own class or for members of other classes. The puppets constructed can be used in different roles as the year progresses.

Here are some sources of help in working with puppetry:

ABC of Puppets (two parts), 16 mm films, 10 minutes each. Bailey Films, 6509 De Longpre Avenue, Hollywood 28, California.

Zechlin, Ruth. *Complete Book of Handcrafts.* Boston: Charles T. Branford Company, 1959.

▶ *Art for world friendship*

Here is an interesting opportunity for correlating art and the language arts with the social studies. Art for World Friendship is a non-profit organization which was begun in Pennsylvania in 1946 by some members of the Women's International League for Peace and Freedom. Its purpose is to extend friendship around the world through the exchange of children's art.

The pictures sent are marked on the back with the name, age, address, and country of the artist. In this way many students find themselves receiving letters from students in other countries who have received their pictures. Sometimes individuals become pen pals or classes exchange letters (through their teachers in the lower grades). Much interest in map study and reading about the country is motivated as children have a real reason for finding out where these friends live in relation to our own country and what that country is like.

This is an activity in which children of all ages are encouraged to participate (pre-school through high school). The pictures can be informative, telling about our way of living. They might, for example, be pictures of the children in their daily school activities or a group of pictures might depict the things we do at home.

An interesting discussion will develop as the group decides on what sorts of pictures they should send. The students should be led to realize that their contributions will be representing the United States abroad. (The organization makes only one limitation on the content of the pictures sent—pictures of war are not accepted.)

In exchange for sending pictures, your class will receive a group of pictures from abroad so that each child who sent a picture will have a picture made by a child his own age from another country. These pictures, too, will bear a name and address to which the child can write. If your class is interested in a particular country, you can specify the country so that, if possible, you will receive drawings from that area.

Information and application forms can be obtained at this address:

> Mrs. Frederick W. Muller, Chairman
> Art for World Friendship
> 51 West 8th Street
> Media, Pennsylvania

Pictures are to be limited in size to anything under 18x22 inches, and are to be *unmounted*. Any non-smearing medium is acceptable (crayon, water color, tempera) and participation may be any time during the year.

As the organization's brochure states: "A universal language—understood by all—pictures can, and do, overcome barriers created by the difference of speech. . . . Children learn that basically their interests, their needs, and their desires are the same as those of children all over the world."

▶ The traveling classroom

As your class begins its study of a geographic area or a period in history, let your classroom help to transport the children to that locality or period of time. Suppose, for example, that your class is studying Mexico. There are many interesting ways in which your classroom can reflect this study so that the student entering the room will immediately experience some of the atmosphere of this country.

• *Pictures.* One of the first ways to bring Mexico to your classroom is to display pictures, especially large ones like the travel posters which may be obtained from an embassy or travel agency (See Chapter 7). Students may bring pictures from home, and the school picture file should also contain many. After students have gained some background knowledge of this country, they will be drawing and painting pictures of this area.

• *Realia.* Borrow realia from the families in your room and any others who might lend serapes, musical instruments such as maracas, castanets, and other articles obtained in Mexico. If your school has a Resource File, this file will list persons willing to lend such realia.

| GREEN | WHITE | RED |

MEXICAN FLAG

• *Flags.* Make a Mexican flag (look in large dictionary under "flag") which can be hung on the wall. Use crayon on unbleached muslin or crayon on a large sheet of white drawing paper.

• *Costumes and Dolls.* The girls will enjoy making costumes for their smaller dolls. These can be made at home or at school if time permits. A good book to help with this type of activity is by Helen J. Fletcher, *The See and Do Book of Dolls and Doll Houses* (New York: H. S. Stuttman Co., 1959).

Simple costumes can be made for the students to wear when participating in creative dramatics during their study of Mexico. The boys might wear a colorful serape from crepe paper which is sewn together by hand. Girls can construct bright aprons also of crepe paper.

• *Language.* Introduce the students to the language of the country. In this case Spanish words would be learned (for less familiar languages you would need to probe your community for help). Students will enjoy learning to count from one to ten—*uno, dos, tres, cuatro, cinco, seis, siete, ocho, nueve, diez.* They will also enjoy the color words—*Los Colores:*

rojo—red	*negro*—black
amarillo—yellow	*blanco*—white
azul—blue	*violeto*—purple
verde—green	*moreno*—brown

Words for common objects around the classroom can be printed on cards with a felt pen and mounted around the room. The card containing the word *ventana* would, for example, be placed near the window. Number and color words can be mounted on a bulletin board or chart with appropriate explanations of their meanings. Words which we have borrowed directly from the Spanish language should be discussed and also words that appear the same in both our languages because of a common Latin derivation:

46

Words Borrowed	Common Derivation
rodeo	animal
pronto	familiar
bonanza	fatal
pinto	brutal
San, Santa (in city names)	hotel

• *Songs.* Introducing the language immediately suggests the learning of a Spanish song like *La Cucaracha* (The Cockroach), *Cièlo Lindo* (Beautiful Heaven), or any number of others which commonly appear in songbooks. A record that is helpful in teaching songs with correct pronunciation is called *Cantemos* (*Let's Sing*). (Penny Press, 366 Greenwich St., New York, New York)

• *Dances.* The children can wear their costumes while learning a Mexican folkdance. Your music consultant or a member of the community might be able to help you teach the dance. An easy Spanish dance for elementary school children is *La Raspa.* Two excellent sources are as follows:

Mooney, Gertrude, *Mexican Folk Dances for American Schools.* Coral Gables, Florida: University of Miami Press.

Johnston, Edith, *Regional Dances of Mexico.* (records) Banks Upshaw Co., 905 Calhoun, Dallas, Texas.

• *Records.* You can find numerous records of Spanish music which a small committee of students could play before school, during free periods, or while students are working on, for example, an art project. When a record is being played, the name of the selection, the composer and the performing artist should be written on the board so that students will become somewhat acquainted with this music. Favorites can be repeated by request.

• *Maps.* Students will draw maps of the area. A large map of Mexico can be outlined on butcher paper (use the opaque projector to enlarge a small one). Cities can be located as well as land forms such as mountains, lakes, rivers and historical points of interest. More detailed maps may be made by individual students to explore specific areas such as Mexico City.

• *Equivalent Names.* Children can make name cards bearing their *Spanish names.* Paul's name, for example, would be Pablo; Mary's would be María. Children whose names are not typical in Spanish could choose a Spanish name if they wished.

• *Dioramas.* They can be made by all of the students or by a small group which has extra time to explore special topics. The individual dioramas may depict scenes of Mexican life, early explorations of Mexico, the lives of well-known people in Mexico, or historical sites of interest.

• *Puppet Shows.* The puppet show can be used to depict stories of Mexican life. As described earlier in this chapter, students can make simple puppets with which to illustrate an understanding of the culture of Mexico. They can use some Spanish expressions in the dialogue such as *por favor* (please) or *gracias* (thank you).

Other activities which will increase the students' understanding of Mexico's land and people are listed here:

- Make a *mural* depicting, perhaps, a festival scene.
- Write *stories and poetry* about Mexico's people and their history.
- Read *books* (fiction and non-fiction) about Mexico.
- *Write* to children in Mexico:
    Children's Plea for Peace
    World Affairs Center, the University of Minnesota
    Minneapolis, Minnesota.

    International Friendship League
    40 Mount Vernon Street
    Boston 8, Massachusetts.
- Have a *speaker* who has been to Mexico.
- Feature Mexico in the study of *current events*.
- Show *films, filmstrips,* and *slides.*
- Make a 24 hour clock.
- Make a *piñata.*

6

WORKING WITH
MAPS AND GLOBES

This chapter will concern itself primarily with the presentation of different techniques for teaching map skills and understandings. The selection of the particular techniques described is based on: (1) student involvement, (2) differing levels of ability and skills, (3) construction of materials, (4) subject correlation, (5) both individual and group work, and (6) open-ended assignments. The following ideas are ones designed and selected to increase the students' knowledge and interest in the study of maps and globes:

- The Hot Spot
- Adopt-A-Ship
- Create a Country
- Constructing Maps and Globes

► The hot spot

An idea which helps correlate maps and globes with the study of current events is the so-called Hot Spot map. This map uses large red thumbtacks placed in a location indicating a Hot Spot or an area where crucial events are occurring. Enlarge regular sized thumbtacks by gluing on a one-inch circle of red construction paper. These thumbtacks may be numbered to correspond to newspaper articles on display, or strings may connect the thumbtack locator with the article. Thus the map and the indicators can be part of a current events bulletin board.

The Hot Spot map serves to sensitize pupils to areas of contemporary interest. It serves to heighten pupil interest in current events and is often the beginning of a fruitful discussion. When a number of Hot Spots occur, for example, in a particular location in Africa, the question might well be raised why this area of the world has more than its share of difficulties at this time.

Students may in this way begin not only to read maps but to interpret them and to acquire some degree of competence in locational skills. The type of map focuses on current events study and at the same time features the study of geographic locations. It also encourages students to contribute news articles.

This technique can be developed by the entire class or it can be handled by a small committee. Several advanced students may be in charge changing articles, finding locations, and reporting to the class at intervals.

▶ Adopt-a-ship

One excellent idea that correlates map study with language arts is that of Adopting a Ship. The basic description in brief is that the class or a group from the class corresponds with the captain of a merchant ship that is sailing from port to port. This correspondence with the captain provides an opportunity to plot his course on a map in the classroom and follow the ship's route as it moves to different ports of call.

In his letters the captain describes his position and gives short descriptions of the areas he is visiting. He also answers questions asked by the students in their letters to him. He may at times send maps and small realia appropriate to the locales.

The Adopt-A-Ship Plan can be utilized with the whole class participating, dividing the class into committees including one that will construct a map with a small ship to move as the course of the ship is plotted, another committee to supervise correspondence, another to do research about the areas reached by the ship and to prepare background information for the class.

This activity can also be conducted by a group of gifted students in the class. They might conduct the research, handle correspondence, and map the route of the ship, making periodic reports to the class which would benefit from the work done by these students.

This activity carries such interest that the route of the ship adopted by one class might be plotted in a central location in the school so that all students could note its progress. The school newspaper or the daily news report could carry informative items about the ship which the class is following.

Letters of application and additional information may be obtained by a teacher from this address: Adopt-A-Ship Plan, Suite 2639, 17 Battery Place, New York 4, New York.

No individual person may adopt a ship; the project must be done by school class members under the supervision of a teacher. The teacher must file the application and supervise the class participation. The period of correspondence is from September through May, but the number of ships available each year is limited so it is wise to apply well in advance.

▶ Create a country

One of the most imaginative ideas concerned with the study of maps and globes is that of creating a country. Many aspects of the study of maps and globes become rather mechanical and routine. The creation of a country, on the other hand, opens new areas that are fascinating to the student as he learns map skills in a different way.

The students, as individuals or as a class, create a small country, deciding on the specifics in terms of area, geographic location, topography, climate, the people, the history, and government. This technique is an open-ended activity in which the extent of development depends on the grade level, the interest of the individual students, the purposes of the teacher, and the amount of time available. It also offers an opportunity to correlate the social studies with other subject areas such as the language arts, art, science, and music. It can involve the use of a variety of skills on the part of the student—writing, drawing, map construction, speaking, and dramatizing.

The best way to describe this technique and to illustrate its use at different levels of development is to set up three levels telling what might be involved at each.

• *Level One.* Class members first draw an aerial view of their imaginary countries. Before the students begin drawing, the teacher should set the stage with a discussion of what they are going to do. It should be clear that they are going to create a country, one that is wholly imaginary. The students should be led to think of the various geographic elements that might exist in a country, such as rivers, lakes, mountains, and cities. They should be encouraged to think in terms of a small country which would be less complicated and more easily described. A small island country is, for these reasons, sometimes used.

After the initial picture is completed the students can write short descriptions of their countries. They should choose names for their countries. The better descriptions can be read to the class while the discoverer displays his aerial view of the country. This simple

51

picture represents the first step in map study and can be carried out in the primary grades.

• *Level Two*. Let us now assume that the students have progressed through the procedure described in Level One.

The students at Level Two can proceed by drawing a map of their imaginary country. The maps may be freehand, relief, or flat projections drawn to scale. The young geographers can study map skills while using symbols, showing directions, the scale used, and topography. The country can also now be located in the world setting through the use of latitude and longitude. The location of the country will determine the climate, rainfall, type of growth, and so forth.

• *Level Three*. At the highest level of development the class as a whole "discovers" one country (perhaps the best of those prepared individually). Together they decide on general information about the country. The basic data needed includes: area and geographic location, population size, the name of the country.

After the class determines the general characteristics of the imaginary country, the group can divide into a number of study teams. Various teams of scholars will prepare information pertaining to this new country and its society. The anthropologists, for example, will develop the imaginary people who inhabit the land. They will decide on the origin and the racial characteristics of the people. Other scholars will explore other aspects of the society and the country:

- Anthropologists (people, origin, racial characteristics)
- Political scientists (government, constitution, foreign relations)
- Geographers (topography, cartography)
- Economists (industries, organization of business, monetary system)
- Educators (school system—all levels)
- Linguists (language)
- Sociologists (institutions like the family; way of living)
- Mathematicians (number system)
- Creative artists (folklore, literature, art, music)
- Communicators (newspaper, radio, television)

A number of specific activities will be developed as appropriate by each of the study groups. Some suggestions include the following:

1. Make a national flag.
2. Write a national motto and a pledge of allegiance.
3. Write a national anthem.

4. Construct a large relief map.
5. Write legends.
6. Write poetry and short stories.
7. Draw pictures of scenes, people, activities.
8. Map rainfall, products, population, etc.
9. Write a newspaper.
10. Design coins and stamps.

A good way to demonstrate the interdependence of the elements of a society is to lead the students to discover the necessity for the coordination of their efforts in developing the various areas being studied. The study groups will need to consult in order to avoid conflicts as they plan each part of the society which they are creating for this imaginary country. The economists, for example, will need to confer with the mathematicians before developing a monetary system, and the sociologists will confer with the anthropologists as they describe the people and their way of living.

► *Constructing maps and globes*

This section will describe four types of maps which can be constructed in the classroom: (1) Walk-Around map, (2) Flat projection, (3) Relief map, and (4) Globe.

• *The Walk-Around Map.* An example of one of the first maps used in the elementary school is the walk-around or walk-through map. This map can be developed as a result of a short excursion or walk around the school and its vicinity. It is particularly appropriate for the primary grades as pupils begin exploring their community.

The map usually consists of boxes, cartons, and blocks placed on the floor to indicate buildings and houses. These boxes can be painted to represent various types of buildings. Masking tape is often used to indicate the roads, streets, and intersections. The children construct traffic lights of shoe boxes mounted on dowel rods set in cans of gravel or sand. As the name given this type of map indicates, children can walk along the streets, passing buildings and stopping at the street crossings.

It is a useful device for teaching safety concepts and for role playing—the policeman, ladies walking down the street, or the storekeeper whose store is on Main Street.

The advantage of this map is that while it is somewhat abstract, it still remains a pictorial representation of a real area which is being described. The teacher can vary the amount of space required for this map project. If space is limited, a map of this nature might be constructed on a large table or a sand table. The boys and girls can assist in making houses, trees, roadways and other landmarks in the school area.

• *The Flat Projection.* The next stage in the use of maps is the representation of an area on a flat sheet of paper with the children locating their own homes and other landmarks. Students can trace their routes from home to school.

• *Freehand Maps.* The freehand map is sketched by pupils of areas with which they are familiar. This may be the vicinity of the school, an area visited on a field trip, or the school building itself. The students might draw a map, for example, after visiting the airport. A good way to develop one of these maps is to take a special trip specifically for the purpose of mapping the terrain. Students in this way may encounter interesting land forms, such as a hill or a river.

These freehand sketch maps will show development and progress in two directions: (1) from pictorial representation to abstract symbols and (2) from approximate or no scale to the use of a specific scale. A point to keep in mind in using freehand sketch maps is that they should never be allowed to become too complicated. The map should emphasize only the important features of the area and should be of a small enough area to be completely familiar to the students.

This type of map can include the concepts of the cardinal directions as well as the use of simple symbols. The extent to which these maps are developed depends on the level of sophistication of the students. These maps are also dependent upon the pupils' experiencing or viewing areas to be mapped, for they evolve from direct experience. In constructing these maps directly from experience the students are functioning cartographers.

• *Copying Flat Maps.* When a more accurate outline of a country is needed for use in map study, it is sometimes practical to have students copy a commercially prepared outline map. The opaque projector can be used very successfully for this purpose. This projector will project any opaque material onto a large sheet of paper fastened to the wall or bulletin board so that students can trace the outline. The size of the map can be controlled by moving the projector farther away to enlarge the projection and closer to the paper to secure a smaller representation.

Another method of obtaining accurate outline maps is to trace a map from one of the large flat commercial wall maps. These methods are particularly functional when a large outline map of a continent is needed for a relief map.

• *The Relief Map.* The use of the relief map has many justifications, but its primary function is that it shows or demonstrates to the student the surface features of an area. Following are ten steps that will help the teacher in supervising the construction of relief maps:

1. Make a large outline map of the area to be shown. The outline map can be made by the use of either the tracing method or the opaque projector enlargement.

2. On this paper map note the features that are to be shown, such as mountain ranges, valleys, flat plains, and lakes.

3. Draw an outline of the paper map directly on the board (hardboard, plywood, thick cardboard) which will hold the relief map.

4. Tack small brads, nails, or tacks on the board to indicate the heights to be shown.

5. Prepare modeling material according to the recipe given here:

> 2 cups table salt
> 1 cup cornstarch
> 1 cup water (Paint or food coloring may be added)

> Directions: Mix salt and cornstarch thoroughly, then add water and mix. Cook slowly over low heat, stirring constantly. When mixture forms stiff lump, let it cool. Knead and use. Hardens when dry. May be stored in cool place, if to be used next day.

6. Apply mixture directly to board, checking the paper reference map which indicates land forms to be included on the map, as well as tacks showing varying heights. Tongue depressors can be used to spread the modeling mixture over the surface and to sculpture the land forms.

7. Allow several days for the map to dry thoroughly.

8. Color the relief map to highlight land forms. Use the standard colors found on relief maps.

9. A compass should be drawn and mounted at one corner of the map. Names of cities, rivers, countries, lakes and other markings can be written on small paper pennants which are mounted on steel straight pins pressed into the map surface.

10. The map should be shellacked or varnished to preserve the finished surface.

One large relief map can represent a project for the entire class with small groups of students handling different parts of the procedure. At other times you may wish to have committees working on smaller relief maps of areas being studied. If, for example, your class is studying the United States, one group might map the Pacific

Northwest while another concentrates on New England. Another possibility is the making of small relief maps by each individual pupil. Each might, for instance, be mapping one specific state.

• *The Globe.* Globes can also be constructed by the individual child. There are certain advantages to this type of construction. The student actually handles the globe. He can use his individual globe during class discussion locating countries so that concepts of distance and direction are developed to the fullest extent. Handling the globe rather than a flat map has the advantage of helping to eliminate the distorted view of the earth as a flat expanse of land and water.

As each student develops his own globe, locating countries, rivers, continents, oceans, the poles, the equator, lines of longitude and latitude, he more fully understands Columbus's revolutionary idea of sailing west to get to the East, what people mean when they mention crossing the equator, or why there is a reversal of seasons betwen the northern and southern hemispheres. He discovers the need for latitude and longitude lines.

To construct individual globes you will need the following materials: heavy grade round balloons (1 per student); wheat paste; shellac or varnish; newspaper; tempera paints.

Following are the instructions for constructing individual globes with newspaper strips:

1. Inflate the balloons to the desired size—12 to 18 inches is a good diameter for the globe. (Use an inflating device such as available for air mattresses.) Attach heavy cord to the balloon to provide a hanging arrangement for the finished globe.

2. Mix wheat paste to a thick consistency. (Several pans of the paste should be available so a number of students may work at once.)

3. Cut newspaper into three-inch strips which are tapered to a point at one end. Dip each strip into the paste and apply it to the globe.

4. After applying two layers of newspaper, hang the globe on a rope or wire which has been stretched across the back of the room and allow to dry overnight. (Hang globes over a thick layer of newspapers.)

5. Add three more layers of newspaper. If the continents are to be painted, finish the globe with a layer of white tissue strips.

6. Mark continents and oceans after lines of longitude and latitude and the poles have been determined. If a relief globe is desired, use a recipe of the salt and cornstarch mixture given for

relief maps. (Before applying this mixture, shellac the globe so moisture will not cause it to sag.)

TIP: Before marking the globes have one student hold his globe in front of the class. Pin a piece of colored construction paper on any spot of this unmarked globe. Ask students to describe the location of this marker. When they have agreed on its location, turn the unmarked ball upside down. Now where is the marker? Repeat this operation several times to illustrate the fact that an unmarked globe is of little value, for although the marker remains in the same place on the globe, the ball itself changes position. This activity illustrates the need for lines of latitude and longitude which help us locate places. These lines can then be placed on the globes.

When all markings have been placed on the globe, give them several coats of shellac. The finished globes can then be used in classroom work. Later at home they can be hung in the student's bedroom for continued use.

7

FINDING
INSTRUCTIONAL MATERIALS

As you begin to plan any unit or area of study, one of the first problems which you face is the gathering of sufficient, good instructional material. There are many different types of material available and numerous sources to consider. Read through this list of the various types of instructional materials available so as to get an idea of what sorts of things you may expect to use:

- Texts and supplementary texts
- Reference books (encyclopedias, atlases, *Readers' Guide*)
- Enrichment books (fiction and non-fiction)
- Books for the teacher
- Vertical file pamphlets, clippings
- Periodicals (magazines, newspapers)
- Films, filmstrips
- Slides, Viewmaster slides
- Records, tapes
- Television and radio programs (AM and FM)
- Maps, globes
- Charts, pictures
- Models, exhibits, realia

It is common for the individual school to supply texts, maps and globes, some records, and library books. School districts usually have a system also for the borrowing of films. Beyond this supply, however, the teacher must often use ingenuity in finding materials to develop a unit of study.

What are the sources of additional instructional materials? There are a number to be explored: (1) the teacher herself, (2) libraries, (3) colleges and universities, and (4) agencies supplying free and inexpensive materials.

► The teacher herself

• *The Idea File.* Any teacher will find the Idea File indispensable. This file can be started at any time and is usually kept on 4x6 cards, lined or unlined. Categories are established according to the teacher's needs. Suggested categories to be included are:

Games	Bulletin Board
Arts and Crafts	Gifted Child
Reading	Current Events
Writing	Addresses
Maps and Globes	Classroom Management

As the teacher reads or hears of an interesting idea, she notes it briefly, but completely, on a card and files it under the appropriate category. When she needs an idea in any area, she can quickly glance at the cards in one category to find a good idea to suit her purposes. When beginning a new area of study in the social studies, she will check her file for addresses of organizations which will supply pictures and brochures about that particular area.

• *The Picture File.* The Picture File, too, is invaluable (see Chapter 3). Some schools maintain a central file of pictures, but more commonly the teacher must depend on her own supply. In order to develop a good file of pictures, the teacher must constantly be alert. Students can help with clipping, trimming, and filing the pictures so that they are readily available, for a set of wonderful pictures is of no use if you cannot find the right picture when you want it.

If desired, choice pictures may be mounted, but be sure to mount on one neutral color, such as white, tan or gray, so these pictures can be used with any color scheme. Extensive mounting is not recommended; unmounted pictures can be more easily filed in folders and will appear mounted if you pin them on colored construction paper when used in a display.

Magazines which contain particularly good pictures are the following: *Look, Life, Holiday, National Geographic, Ideals, Arizona Highways.*

► Libraries

If you live in a metropolitan area, you will have many library facilities available. Rural areas, too, are serviced by city or county libraries. Investigate your own locality to discover what library facilities are available to you. Libraries you may expect to find include: (1) the school library, (2) the city public library, (3) the college library, (4) the county library, and (5) the state department of education library.

• *The School Library*. No longer is the school library merely a collection of books. The school library is more and more becoming an instructional materials center, supplying all sorts of audio-visual materials for the teachers' use. If you have a school library, check its card catalog to determine what materials are available from this source. You may also arrange to borrow materials from other school libraries in your school system. Consult the high school librarian to see if this would be convenient.

Is there a professional library located in your school? Here is a supply of books, pamphlets, and materials meant specifically for the teachers' use. You may find helpful references for the area you plan to study. You may also find books listing sources of free and inexpensive materials (discussed later in this chapter).

• *The City Public Library*. Public libraries are usually glad to help any teacher who consults them. You should visit the public library in your vicinity to see what facilities are available to you and to your students. Frequently the teacher is permitted to borrow classroom quantities of books. The students in your class should be encouraged to use the public library when doing any research. These libraries often maintain sizable record collections and picture files. They can supply back issues of magazines which may contain pertinent articles listed in *Readers' Guide*.

• *The College Library*. Colleges and universities are very much interested in helping the public school teacher. Their library facilities are usually available to any member of their community. Young students may not be permitted to check out materials, but they are welcome to use the library reference room which contains more specialized reference tools than those practical for the public or school library.

Too, college libraries frequently maintain a curriculum laboratory which is directed toward the teachers' needs. Here you may find a variety of texts, resource units, and so forth.

• *The County Library*. In rural areas it has been found practical to pool resources in a centralized instructional materials center which services a large number of schools. In this way items which are too expensive for the individual school can be purchased and shared. If your county maintains this type of service, it will be an excellent source of materials of infinite variety.

• *The State Department of Education*. Many state departments of education issue helpful materials for the teachers' use. Check with your librarian or directly by mail to find out what services your department of education offers. They may lend films or supply teaching aids.

► Colleges and universities

We have already mentioned the possibility of using college library facilities. Colleges and universities also offer other types of assistance. The faculty members in the various departments are often willing to help the public school teacher. They are excellent sources of information either through personal interview or by correspondence. You may also ask a professor to speak to your class about the topic being studied.

Music and art departments may have special materials available. If you are studying a specific country, for example, you might get suggestions about studying the music and art of that country. Some art departments have paintings and prints available for borrowing or rental. Audio-visual centers at the college can supply film catalogs and information about various teaching devices.

► Free and inexpensive materials

Many public and private agencies make available to the teacher various types of learning materials. For some of these materials there is a small fee, but others are free to the teacher. Pamphlets, books, samples, pictures, reports, maps, films and filmstrips— these are some kinds of material provided by government agencies, travel offices, private industry, foreign embassies, and various associations.

These materials have a number of advantages. They are usually up to date in covering a particular topic. For this reason they often supply information not yet available in book form. Many of the materials, such as pictures, maps, and posters, aid in the making of attractive bulletin board displays.

These items can be added to the teacher's or the school's file of instructional aids, thereby enlarging the source of information about any topic. Material should be examined for bias and excessive advertising before using it in the classroom.

When the teacher requests materials from any source, she should state the purpose for which the material is to be used. To be certain of receiving the items requested, write on school stationery. When a number of sources are being contacted, however, it has proved successful to use a duplicated postal card which can be provided by the school office. The teacher requesting the material should sign her name on each card.

61

Dear Sir:

Your name and address were listed in _____

_____. May we please have copies

of the following _____

_____ for use in the classroom.

Thank you very much.

> Teacher
> School
> Address

- *Books and Pamphlets.* There are a number of books and pamphlets which list names and addresses of agencies that supply free or inexpensive materials for teachers. Listed here are some of those which might be considered for purchase by the individual teacher or the school library if they are not already available:

> Cardozo, Peter, *A Wonderful World for Children.* Bantam Books, 271 Madison Avenue, New York 16, New York. (A paperback for the general public.)
>
> George Peabody College for Teachers, *Free and Inexpensive Learning Materials.* Nashville 5, Tennessee. (Excellent source for the teacher or librarian.)
>
> Kenworthy, Leonard S., *Free and Inexpensive Materials on World Affairs.* Brooklyn College, Brooklyn 10, New York. (Special subject area.)
>
> Miller, Bruce, *Sources of Free and Inexpensive Teaching Aids.* (Pamphlet published by author: Riverside, California.)
>
> Schain, Robert L. and Murray Polner, *Where to Get and How to Use Free and Inexpensive Teaching Aids.* Prentice-Hall, Englewood Cliffs, New Jersey. (The only book available that tells not only where to get materials but also specifically how to evaluate and use them. Lesson plans, do's and don't's, and so forth.)

- *Magazines.* Some magazines carry regular features listing free and inexpensive materials available. Listed here are some magazines which can be checked: *Audio-Visual Instruction, Booklist, Educational Screen and Audio-Visual Guide, Grade Teacher, Instructor, National Education Association Journal,* your state *Education Association Journal.*

- *Sources for Particular Geographic Areas.* Listed here are representative sources of learning materials which are particularly appropriate for the social studies teacher. Only free materials have been included in this selected list.

AFRICA

> Information Service of South Africa. 655 Madison Avenue, New York 21, New York.
>
> East Africa Tourist Travel Association. 6 East 45th Street, New York 17, New York. (Kenya, Uganda, Tanganyika)

United Arab Republic Tourist Office. 2300 Decatur Place, N.W., Washington 8, D.C. (Egypt)

ASIA

Embassy of Indonesia. 2020 Massachusetts Avenue, N.W., Washington 6, D.C.

Chinese News Service. 1270 Sixth Avenue, New York 20, New York

Japan Tourist Association. 45 Rockefeller Plaza, New York 20, New York.

Information Service of India, Embassy of India. 2107 Massachusetts Avenue, N.W., Washington 6, D.C.

Israel Office of Information. 11 East 70th Street, New York 21, New York.

Consulate-General of Japan, Information Office. 3 East 54th Street, New York 22, New York.

AUSTRALIA

Australian News and Information Bureau. 636 Fifth Avenue, New York 20, New York.

EUROPE

Casa de Portugal. 447 Madison Avenue, New York 22, New York.

Danish Information Service. 588 Fifth Avenue, New York 36, New York.

Finnish National Travel Office. 10 East 40th Street, New York 16, New York.

Press and Information Service, Royal Greek Embassy. 120 East 56th Street, New York 22, New York.

Italian State Tourist Office. 21 East 51st Street, New York 22, New York.

British Information Service. 30 Rockefeller Plaza, New York 20, New York.

French Embassy, Cultural Division. 972 Fifth Avenue, New York 21, New York.

German Embassy, Information Office. 1742-44 R Street, N.W., Washington 9, D.C.

Netherlands Information Service. 711 Third Avenue, New York 17, New York.

Spanish Embassy, Cultural Relations. 2700 15th Street, N.W., Washington 5, D.C.

Royal Swedish Embassy. Washington 8, D.C.

NORTH AMERICA (OTHER THAN U.S.)

Mexican Government Tourist Department. 630 Fifth Avenue, New York 20, New York.

Canadian Government Travel Bureau. Ottawa, Canada.

Field Enterprises Educational Corporation. Merchandise Mart Plaza, Chicago 54, Illinois. (Mexico and others. Write for list.)

SOUTH AMERICA

Brazilian Embassy. 3007 Whitehaven Street, N.W., Washington 8, D.C.

Pan American Union. Office of Publications, Washington 6, D.C.

United Fruit Company, Educational Department. Pier 3, North River, New York 6, New York.

UNITED NATIONS

U.S. Committee for the United Nations. 816 21st Street, N.W., Washington 6, D.C.

UNESCO, United Nations. New York 17, New York.

Alaskan Division of Tourism and Economic Development. Room 310, Alaska Office Building, Juneau, Alaska.

Hawaii Visitors Bureau. 2051 Kalakaua Avenue, Honolulu 15, Hawaii.

Indian Rights Association, 1505 Race Street, Philadelphia 3, Pennsylvania.

Haskell Institute. Lawrence, Kansas. (Indians)

Empire State Observatory. Fifth Avenue and 34th Street, New York, New York.

U. S. Treasury Department, Information Service. Washington 25, D.C.

Veterans of Foreign Wars of the United States. Broadway at 34th Street. Kansas City 11, Missouri. (U. S. flag information)

- *Sources for Industry Topics*

National Coal Association, Education Section. 808 15th Street, N.W., Washington 5, D.C.

American Forest Product Industries, Inc. 1816 N Street, N.W., Washington 6, D.C.

American Petroleum Institute. 50 West 50th Street, New York 20, New York.

U.S. Steel Corporation, Public Relations Department. 71 Broadway, New York 6, New York.

Standard Oil Company of California. Box 3495, San Francisco 20, California.

General Motors Corporation, Educational Relations Section. Warren, Michigan.

- *Sources for Transportation Topics*

Ford Motor Company, Information Services. Dearborn, Michigan.

United Aircraft Corporation. East Hartford 8, Connecticut.

United Air Lines, School and College Service. Chicago 38, Illinois.

Pan American World Airways System. 28-19 Bridge Plaza North, Long Island City 1, New York.

American Merchant Marine Institute. 11 Broadway, New York 4, New York.

The Association of American Railroads. Washington 6, D.C.

General Motors, Public Relations Department. Detroit 2, Michigan.

American Trucking Association, Inc. 1424 16th Street, N.W., Washington 6, D.C.

Automobile Manufacturers' Association. New Center Building, Detroit 2, Michigan.